Vagabonds

Richard Baker

Contents

'My body lies, but still I roam'
-    Metallica, Wherever I may roam

1. Introduction

For as long as I remember I've always loved all kinds of music. I was brought up in a household full of old records, cassettes and CD's. When I was 7 or 8 years of age I bought a twin deck portable cassette player from Argos with my birthday money so that I could make my own radio shows on. I even did introductions to each track like I heard everyone on the radio do.

When I was around ten years old I remember being sat in my parents living room listening to a tape on my Dad's beautiful stacked amplifier set up with his headphones on. My Dad walked over to me and offered to show me how to use the CD player. This was a rite of passage. Up until this point I'd not been allowed to touch or use the CD player.

He showed me the ins and outs of how to use the machine, which buttons to select on the amplifier, how to load and unload a CD from the five-disc changer and how to skip through. He then pointed me towards his tower of CD's and asked me to go ahead and choose one to listen to. I picked up CD after CD deliberating on which one would be my first CD to listen to. I finally settled on an all-black

CD with an embossed black snake in the corner. I didn't know it at the time, but this CD would change my life. I couldn't see the band name anywhere but thought it looked cool.

I carefully placed it in the CD changer as I'd been shown and hit play. I put my dads expensive headphones on and heard the cool opening riff to Enter Sandman surround my ears, plinked away on a clean guitar, followed by the thunderous drums, which crescendoed into the main riff. I thought my head was going to explode, what on earth was this!!! I'd never heard anything like it before and I was immediately hooked. I turned it up loud and grinned from ear to ear. This was amazing.

When I hit secondary school a friend of mine asked me if I wanted to learn to play drums. My school offered a select amount of lessons to people that were interested but you had to have two people per lesson in order for it to make fiscal sense for the school to subsidise them. For some reason my friend asked me and by doing so changed the course of my life from thereafter. I said yes because it meant I could get out of some school lessons once a week to play drums, sounded like a no brainer!

By the time it got to my next birthday I was completely absorbed in the thought of being a professional drummer. I didn't care about school or anything other than drumming and skateboarding. I'd managed to scrape together enough money to buy a second-hand drum kit a friend of a friend was selling; I just had to convince my parents. My Dad was cool with it, my Mum was frosty to the idea but eventually relented, probably thinking it was just a phase. I set it up in the garage around my Dads tools directly underneath the onions he used to store in there that would periodically drop from where he was hanging them and land on me while I relentlessly thumped away at my kit. It didn't sound anywhere near as nice as the beautiful expensive kits we had at school, so I taped up the heads with gaffer and filled the bass drum with blankets until it sounded half decent. So that I could completely zone out and pretend I was just like the drummers I was hearing on my headphones I used to crank the volume up to maximum and hit the drums as hard as I could. This led to me developing a loud aggressive playing style that I still use today and definitely contributed to my tinnitus.

At the tender age of fifteen I started gigging with bands at local venues and became engrossed in the local music scene, which was thriving at the time. Myspace was just beginning to be utilised as a promotional tool and I was being exposed to new music everywhere I went. Playing gigs, going to gigs and learning songs on drums became my world. Everything else was a necessary evil, distant noise that was just getting in the way of me doing what I was passionate about.

I maintained my passion for music right through College, University and it landed me a job working for a local events management company. Which gave me the flexibility to work in the industry I loved whilst also pursuing a career in creating music.

Eventually I had some moderate success playing drums in a band called Wraiths. Wraiths were self-branded as 'Hell metal for demons'. We were (and still are) from the North of England and utilised the grim backdrop of the industrial North as our backdrop to deliver visceral doom metal underpinned by a hard-core mentality. Individually the other two members and I had been around the scene long enough to understand what it takes to take a local act a bit further. Small town music scenes can often have a very small-minded crabs-in-a-bucket mentality if you're not careful and so in order for people to take you seriously you had to have a certain amount of professionalism. We utilised satanic imagery and a bad attitude to develop a brand to back up our music and by doing so began getting booked for shows out of the area very quickly.

Wraiths form the majority of the stories you're about to read. I have many more from tours with other bands that took me on the road with them, but they are their stories to tell. A couple of them get a shout out towards the end though, the ones that wouldn't land anyone in trouble with the law.

Wraiths toured extensively and signed to a small label named Ghost Music, who were a pretty big deal at the time. They put out our second EP and the frustrations behind the release eventually led to our demise. When we get together now to hang out, we often find ourselves recounting these stories and I wanted to get them down on paper as the memories were beginning to fade, as they do, over time. It doesn't help that we were intoxicated for the most part and so I've had to ask the guys to fill in the blanks.

Naturally some names have been left out or changed as I didn't want to throw anyone under the bus, but each memory is true to the best of my recollection.

2. Wraiths first van show - Kendal 13th July 2012

If there's one thing Wraiths were good at, it was selling ourselves and appearing larger than life over the internet. Due to our members past experience in bands we had a pretty good grip on social media and marketing, so we had a music video out before we'd even played a show. When we put our first tracks online, we were asked if we'd like to play a show in a small town called Kendal, just outside of the Lake District. This was our second show ever, and to be playing one out of our home-town so quickly gave us some prestige. It also gave us a chance to fuck up to complete strangers should we need to work out the kinks of our freshly formed set, so we agreed to do it.

Our friends in Hey! Alaska were winding down as a band by this point, but they were still playing shows and owned a van. We asked their driver and good friend of ours Andy if he'd be up for driving our gear and us to Kendal if we paid him. Which, he obliged. I'm sure he was just happy to be out on the road. Andy pretended to be miserable on tour but I knew there was happiness behind that furrowed brow.

The best thing about Hey! Alaska's van was that there were so many seats. They'd converted an old LDV convoy minibus, put beds in the back so they always had somewhere to sleep, rearranged the seats so you could fit nine people in and there was still room for a full backline to be store in the back.

If I remember correctly, we had the full band (four or five of us, we had a guitarist who floated in and out of the band for a short time) Andy, Luke from Hey! Alaska, Phil Pollard from the departed and some tour wives. It was a rite of passage for us of sorts; first gig in a van together, feeling like a professional band. I'd spend years touring in this van with Hey! Alaska, videoing their sets or selling merch, which I loved, but there was always something in me that wished it was me behind the drum kit in my own band and here I was. The other rite of passage with us was Dale.

Initially Wraiths were Rae (vocals) and Charlton's (lead guitar) idea. I lived with Charlton while he was musing about this band and him and Rae were looking for a drummer. I only made sense that I joined. I tweaked some already written drums that Rae and Charlton had demoed. We booked some studio time in and put an ad out for a bassist. We had a few people apply but Dale nailed the tracks on bass and we invited him to the studio to lay it down.

I remember meeting him in the recording studio. He was quiet, awkward and he nailed the songs. He really didn't talk much that day and seemed quite reserved. Wraiths soon brought that out of him for sure.

The second day I'd spent fully with Dale was this trip to Kendal. We were in the van, excited for the show, some of us were drinking and smoking weed. Dale felt he had a point to prove. The rest of us all had pretty big personalities so I can understand him wanting to make a statement. He took it upon himself to try and impress the rest of us and proceeded to down a bottle of red wine. This dudes barely 18 and around 10 stone-ringing wet.

As I'm sure you can imagine we're about halfway to Kendal and it's very obvious he's drank far more than he can handle. We've all done it. To put it lightly, he was fucking hammered. Naturally we thought it was hilarious, poor guy was trying to impress us and instead he ends up with his head swinging all over, barely able to string a sentence together. We moved him so he was next to the window, as we all knew that the next step was vomit. His face went a shade of grey as all of the colour drained from it, uhoh, he was about to erupt. We wound the window down next to him and he *attempted* to throw up out of it. Instead, he covered himself, the duvet he was under and interior of the window. Maybe 5% of it actually went out of the window, our plan failed. It was bright red and we'd have freaked out if he'd drank anything other than red wine. We threw some old rags at him to clean himself up and each tried to stay as far away from him as possible (which, in a van is fairly impossible) still, we could have a good time anywhere. A little sick on our bassist wasn't going to deter us.

Just when we got settled and back into the swing of things the van started to cough and splutter. This was to be a recurring theme throughout Wraiths illustrious career. We pulled over next to a beautiful set of hills to see what was going on. We opened up the bonnet and those of us that pretended to know about engines decided that it was fucked. Great. We all piled out of the van, unsure of what to do until we realise that we're actually about fifteen-minutes walk from the venue. We selfishly left our driver and all-round nice guy Phil Pollard at the side of the road as we picked up all the gear we could carry and began our walk to the venue with pockets full of beers. After many a wrong turn and some aimless wondering (there was a KFC at some point) our hero showed up. It was the van! The AA had managed to fix the problem thank fuck. I honestly don't know what we'd have done. If it had to have been towed I imagine we'd have been left in Kendal with nothing but the clothes on our backs and some musical equipment. Alas, big bertha (as we affectionately named the van) was back to save the day, just in time for us to set up and play.

By this point we were all out of beer and daytime drunk, except Dale who'd sobered up by now. I vaguely recall him looking over at us smugly as we stumbled around clumsily trying to set up our gear. To this day I have no idea how the gig went. I remember being sat behind the drums, playing the first note, then there's a gap, then I remember hitting the final ring out, everyone clapping as Rae thanked the crowd.

After the show we all asked each other how it went and of course only the sober ones could recount it for us, apparently we smashed it, so from that day forward we spent plenty of gigs barely able to speak, or walk thanks to

intoxication yet somehow getting our shit together enough
to smash it on stage, if I may say so myself.

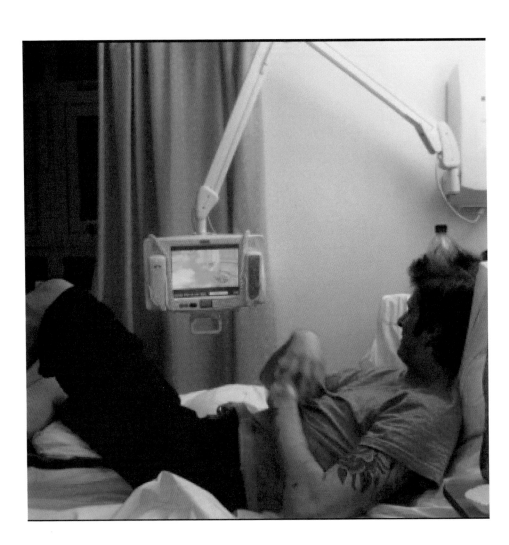

3. Liberties in Town - 29th December 2012

Early on in our career we had two guitarists. Which came in really handy when one of them, Charlton, became severely ill with a back problem. I'm still not quite sure what was wrong with him, but it got so bad that he was in hospital for a long stretch getting vital medication pumped through his chest via something called a Hickman line. I think it was a viral infection in his spine and the Hickman line was a long white cable that protruded from his chest that delivered meds directly to his heart. During the time he was in and out of hospital we had a couple of shows booked but none of us were too bothered about playing them, I'd rather have Charlton back and at full swing ready to kick ass and the other guys felt the same way. Charlton wanted to keep the momentum going and decided to teach our other guitarist a way too mash both guitar lines together in order to pull off the shows. Our other guitarist seemed confident he could pull it off solo so we decided to go ahead with a hometown show at the now defunct, but then 'legendary' Liberties in town.

Preparation was going okay, we sounded passable and were confident with the show. Charlton was messaging us in the days before the gig saying he might be out of hospital in time to play the show. We told him to chill, not rush and get better and not to worry about the show. We all knew he badly wanted to be there but there'd be more gigs. As we got closer to the show he became more and more confident he'd be let out of hospital in time to play the show and so he asked us if we could we take his gear to the show and set it up for him in case it really came down to the wire and he could play the show. It seemed like an odd request at the time, but he was having such a shit time in hospital we obliged him just to make him feel better.

It's gig day, we're all loaded in and about halfway through the opening bands set Rae gets a call. Charlton has busted himself out of hospital and is on the way to the venue. A short while later he appears at the venue looking, well, like he should still be in hospital. He spent most of the gig doubled over in pain, but he was determined to play the show. We set up all his gear for him, put it on stage while he chilled and had a beer then we began our set. As per usual it's absolutely boiling on stage. About halfway through the set Charlton gets so warm he takes his top off, nothing too out of the ordinary for a metal gig, until we realise he's still got half of the tubes hanging out of his fucking chest! This mad bastard must have literally unplugged himself from whatever support he needed and legged it out of the hospital earlier. Like it's nothing he then proceeds to headbang in a circular motion, making all the tubes and attachments hanging out of him swing like a pendulum. It was utterly disgusting, totally amazing and something I'll never forget. I don't think it ever did him any lasting damage and I'm glad to say he eventually made a full recovery from hospital.

After we packed down and hung out for a short while Charlton then headed back to the hospital. God only knows what he told them when he got back there but I'm sure they had questions.

4. Nottingham - 20th May 2013

Every single time I have been to Nottingham something ridiculous has happened. Even before touring it had always been a place that chaos gravitated towards when I was in town. This time around was no different. It was the last day of a tour with a band called Destroyer BC (who we got on with straight away and remain friends with) so we were in a sorry state, we'd been sleeping on floors hungover and living out of a van.

On this particular morning we found a swimming pool that was on the way to the venue. Now, swimming pools are a tour essential, you can get a wash in the showers and some much-needed exercise. We were off to a good start. We'd made decent money on this run, sold a fair amount of merch and so far we'd miraculously been paid at every show we'd played. We decided to treat ourselves and go to an all you can eat Chinese buffet for lunch. After spending most of the run on overpriced petrol station sandwiches and drinking nothing but the cheapest beer we could find this sounded like heaven.

I still remember how it looked from the outside, it was like a brick hut in the middle of nowhere off a small back road. A random spot for a restaurant but we weren't in a position to be too picky. We go out of the van, dusted ourselves off and headed inside. It was exactly as you'd imagine, tonnes of cheap food on hot plates around a huge central table. We piled our plates high and ate until we couldn't move.

Uncomfortably full we piled out of the restaurant, into the van and headed to the venue. I remember it being a beautiful spring day and we were full of the usual excitement, about to play a show but equally excited to be sleeping in our own beds that night. We pulled up to the venue and began unloading gear. The place looked pretty cool, it looked like an old converted working-men's club and we had the entire lounge as our backstage. We checked out the stage, which was a good size, the sound guy seemed to know what he was doing and a fuck load of tickets had been sold. We were in for a rager! Unfortunately, so was my stomach.

I headed back stage to begin setting up my drums. All of a sudden, I was greeted with some vicious sharp stabbing pains in my stomach. I doubled over in agony and curled up into a ball, rolling around and wailing like a madman.

Naturally my band mates thought this was hilarious and presumed I was just acting up. We were all attention seekers in our own ways and would do anything for a laugh, but it quickly became apparent to them that I wasn't fooling around.

I was in real pain and to this day I've not felt anything like it. I stayed on the floor for five or ten minutes longer while my band mates tried to calculate what the cause could be. They began questioning my food choices from the Chinese buffet. We'd hall eaten similar things, right? Wrong, apparently. Turns out everyone else dodged the rice because they thought something didn't look quite right about it. None of the fuckers decided to let me know, so I stuffed my face unknowingly sending my stomach into another dimension.

With barely a seconds notice I had to go to the toilet, immediately. I practically sprinted. I have never moved so fast in my goddamn life. I ran around backstage trying to find the gents like my arse was on fire, which is funny because it was about to be. I eventually found the porcelain, shut the door behind me and breathed a sigh of relief. Until of course, there was no goddamn toilet roll. I should have known. After years on the road my band mates and I had developed an observation of bathrooms. A rule that was simply never broken. There were three things valuable to every road toilet experience. They are:
-A working light
-A working lock
-Some toilet roll

The rule was, that you were guaranteed to be missing one of the three. If you were really unlucky you were missing two of them. Each one leaves you with an individual problem that needs solving on the fly, but I'm sure we can all agree the worst option was to be lacking in the loo roll department.

I text Rae to ask him if he'd do me the honour of sourcing some from another toilet in the venue, thank fully it was a big place so he could do some scouting around. Of course at first he didn't see the message. I tried calling and got nothing. Charlton's phone was off too, great. I must have text Rae a hundred times more and then kept calling him until eventually I heard his signature cackle all the way down the hall and whilst he couldn't hold back his laughter he could at least laugh while walking and he eventually delivered to me the goods.

This toilet became my home for the next few hours. Every time I attempted to leave I would be called back within moments. The minutes ticked by and it got closer and closer to show time and I got the knock I'd been dreading. It was time to go on stage and play. I've never prayed before, but that day I thought about it because nothing was going to stop my bowels from doing what they wanted while I was onstage except for divine intervention.

I tentatively left the bathroom and all of my band mates were trying their hardest to hold it together and not laugh in my face, which was nice of them. They gave me a hand getting my gear on stage, trying my hardest to tense my entire stomach area, we ran a quick line check, gave the sound guy the nod, our intro kicked in and we began our set. My body was tense the whole time; I must have looked like a robot. I didn't dare relax in case the worst happened. It was my nightmare, I'd never come back from soiling myself on stage, I'd have to leave the country. I couldn't wait for the set to end. Around halfway through I felt my intestines shift. Uhoh. You know the feeling, the one you have absolutely no control over. I was terrified. I felt my body relax and I uncontrollably let out the longest, gassiest fart I've ever done. Whatever divine entity was looking down on me that had mercy as thankfully, that was all. Still, I got my band mates back for laughing at me all day.

You see, the stage was big, but apparently not big enough as I looked around, I saw my band members one by one getting hit with the stench. Their faces twist in disgust as the gas slowly drifted across stage making its way towards their nostrils. How they managed to keep playing and not burst out laughing or puke I'll never know, they each shot nasty looks at me as I hit the drums cackling to myself at the current situation. I even remember looking over at Gary Avalanche (our driver for that particular tour) while he was filming parts of the show on his phone. He looked at me, caught a whiff, convulsed and disappeared backstage away from the contamination zone.

Thankfully the rest of the show went on without incident and after we'd packed down I was feeling much better. Cracked a beer and watched some of our good friends in Destroyer BC tear the place up. We said our goodbyes, jumped in the van and headed home. I've never wanted my own bed and shower more.

5. Stuck on a name – Nottingham 15th February 2014

Here we are again, back in the midlands.
Something about this place hates me. For this particular
run of shows we had Gary avalanche driving us again, we
were at the back end of a tour, again, only this time I was
much healthier. Our van however, was not, as we would
soon find out. I remember Gary mentioning something
didn't feel right and we couldn't quite find the venue, so
we pulled over to get our bearings. We found the venue,
which was only a couple of minutes away, jumped in the
van to head over there and the van wouldn't start. Uhoh.
Gary gave it some gas, we all held our breath and after a
couple of starts she fired up again and we were off. We
pulled up outside the venue and decided that instead of
driving to Manchester that night and risking it we'd get the
van home and looked at. If it was something minor we'd
head down to Manchester later in the afternoon or cancel
the show.

We loaded into the venue and had a wicked show.
There were some friends there from other bands, we sold
some merch, drank plenty of beers and we were on our
way. Packed down and ready to roll we remembered the
van's little incident but none of us mention it in case we
jinx the situation. The reality was that we were all thinking
the same thing. We hopped in the van, shut the doors and
held our breath. Gary turned the key and she fired up! Get
the fuck in. The van had some splurts and some stutters,
but she smoothed out and we were on our way. If you've
never been, Nottingham city centre is a fucking nightmare
to drive around. It's full of one-way streets, speed bumps
and constant traffic lights. Each light presented the
potential for our van to break down if we slowed down for
too long and / or had to stay idle for a long time. All we
wanted was to get the van out of the city, on the motorway
and get somewhere near home. We got lucky manoeuvring

around Nottingham skilfully dodging the majority of the red lights and somehow kept the van running. We saw the sign for the slip road and beamed excitedly. We were nearly there. We hit the slip road and are about to pull onto the motorway when it happens.

The engine splutters, there's a grinding noise, the van shuddered and stopped at the side of the fucking slip road. No hard shoulder, nothing, just cars whizzing by at a minimum 70/80mph. We piled out of the van (as is safest to do so) and flipped the hazards on. We had nowhere to stand safely so while Gary was on the phone to the AA to pick us up we were stood about 15 feet away from the back of the van, facing oncoming traffic using the lights on our phones to wave cars across into the next lane. It was absolutely terrifying and not smart, but the alternative was to be decimated by an oncoming vehicle or jump over the side of the bridge. I should point out that the gig probably wrapped at about 11pm so it won't have been much later than that. My point being that it was pitch black. After twenty or so terrifying minutes the police pulled up totally bemused by what was going on. We explained the situation and they pulled out some cones and flashing lights to block the road properly and not have us lunatics stood on the motorway flashing our phones at cars to move over. Thankfully they were pretty cool and were more concerned about our safety than how obviously inebriated we were (except our driver of course). Another twenty minutes roll by and our recovery van turned up. He told us he's only temporary and would only take us to the nearest service station where the next recovery van would pick us up and take us all the way back up North.

We arrived in a service station sometime later, unhooked the van and thanked our police escort and recovery driver. He told us it'd be around half an hour to an hour for our next ride. Service stations are soulless, sad places at the best of times, let alone past midnight when half of the place is closed, but it was better than the side of a motorway, so we made do. We bought some overpriced Burger King while dale smoked a joint, then bought more snacks, then something to drink, chilled in the van, drank some beers. We checked our watches and around 45 minutes had gone by. Fuck. There was no follow-up tow van to be seen. We killed some more time on the gambling machines, spent our loose change on those awful massage chairs. We were running out of beer, this was starting to get serious.

Gary rang the roadside recovery service to see what was going on. It turned out that the guy who dropped us off hadn't bothered to phone ahead and let them know that he wasn't taking us all the way, so we'd dropped off the system. Nice one! We'd all just been killing time for no reason. Obviously it was still going to be some time before another recovery van came and got us but they'd send one right away. Another hour ticked by when finally, another van appeared, hallelujah our lord and saviour! We hooked the van up, forced Dale to sit up front with the driver because he was the youngest and most dispensable if the driver turned out to be a murderer and hit the road. Unfortunately, the tow truck was limited to 50mph on motorways due to the size and nature of them, so it took an insurmountable amount of time to get home. By home, I mean Gary's home, which is where the van needed to be. Gary lived another half an hour from the rest of us, so we had to call in some favours first thing in the morning, unpack the van into several cars and finally, eventually, got to our own beds and didn't talk to each other for about a week.

6. Mosh on the Tyne Festival Newcastle - 31st May 2014

As you may or may not be aware, promoters for small shows sometimes weren't very good at managing money or actually marketing the shows and some of them were just bad people. Often, said promoters made much less money than they had first imagined when they booked a gig. This meant that on many, many occasions promoters would try to get away with not paying one or many of the acts playing their shows. This day was one of those gigs.

In the early days when I was a bit more of a pushover I had let it happen and just bitched about it on the way home, but by now I'd been around the block a bit and had become more confident so often liked to toy with promoters who looked like they were going to attempt to worm their way out of paying us. It got to the point where I was happy to take on the duty of letting these people know that they'd fucked up and to not do it again. I felt like it was my duty, so that if they decided to put shows on again further down the line, other bands didn't have to put up with their shit, like the younger me did in the past.

This particular afternoon was a sunny day, which always led to good spirits. There was nothing better than the sun coming out on a day you have a show, it made load-ins and all of the waiting round much easier. There were bands on all day and we'd purposely arrived a few hours before our set to check the gig out. We were playing in a sports hall in a college complete with bleachers for people to watch from, which looked pretty cool. When our time came, we set up, played, smashed it, sold some t-shirts and begun to pack down. The turnout had been good and the promoter had seemed in good spirits when we arrived and had come over and spoken to us earlier in the day. We'd taken this as a sign that getting paid would be easy, so Charlton and Rae went over to sort the payment out while I began the arduous task of packing my drums away.

They came back over to me laughing not too long later. I asked if they had the cash and they continued laughing saying I was going to have a real good time speaking to this dude, but they'd come with me to provide support. Secretly they just wanted to watch me act all tough knowing that on the inside I was not a mean person. They used to get a kick out of it and would often impersonate me in the van afterwards. We walked over to the entrance where the promoter was sat. Charlton and Rae were slightly behind me as my bouncers, but also holding their laughter at my tough guy act. I introduced myself to the young man and asked if there had been a problem with the money. He looked me in the eyes and said he didn't have enough money to pay us, usual story. There'd not been enough kids at the show to cover the bills. The headliner (Silent Screams) were apparently quite expensive and so he didn't have enough money to pay the rest of us. Rather than take it up with the big boys he decided to fuck over all the smaller bands instead. He tried to feed us the usual bullshit, 'I'll PayPal you it tomorrow' or 'my bank has been frozen, I've lost my card, I'll send you the cash when a new one comes'. Blah Blah Blah. While he was saying all this, he was gesticulating and I noticed he has a Tupperware box in his hand. I looked closer at the box while he fed me his usual bullshit and I could see that it was absolutely bursting at the seams with cash! The nerve on this dude. I started laughing at him and Rae and Charlton did the same when I'd finally realised this guy had the cash.

He stopped talking when I started laughing at him and he seemed confused. I looked him in the eye and said "you realise you're telling me you don't have enough money to pay us, while you're literally waving a box of money under my nose, right?" He looked down at his box full of cash and panicked a bit. He said he only had enough to pay them, no one else. Not on my watch. I told him under no uncertain terms that I wasn't going anywhere until he gave us the cash we had earned, right from his scruffy little Tupperware box. He protested and I simply explained that I didn't want to, but if it came to it I'd just take our money from him by force and there wasn't a fucking thing he could do about it. After a moment of tension, he relented, opened his shitty little Tupperware box and paid us. Naturally I got tortured all the way home by the guys, impersonating my tough guy act.

7. Somewhere in Hull - 8th June 2014

I'm going to try and keep this one relatively anonymous as I do have a lot of respect for the parties involved and it wouldn't be fair on them. We'd played an okay show in Hull as part of a tour and a friend of ours who was involved in the local scene had offered up his house for us to crash at. He explained it was his parents, but it was cool with them. We were very happy with the arrangement. Parents meant cleanliness, working showers and power sockets. All of the essentials.

The show won't go down in the history books, we either had an amazing turn out in Hull or it was quiet, never in the middle. Still, we were a band on the road. We got paid, saw some friends of ours play, drank some beers and hung out. With the van packed and all of our rider beers stashed we piled into the van and headed to our friends house, a ten-minute journey down the road, perfect!

We pulled up to a lovely middle class neighbourhood outside of a well-kept detached house. We looked completely out of place, but we were used to that. Grabbing all of our necessary belongings (phone chargers and beers) we headed inside.

We were presented with two options, crash with everyone in the living room (there's maybe 6 in our touring crew if I remember?) or a very lucky two of us can crash in the loft room. Complete with an actual bed and a duvet. Naturally Rae and I jumped at the chance to sleep on something other than a floor, so we chose that room before anyone else could protest. We headed upstairs and dumped our gear, set up our sleeping arrangements before heading to the garden for some beers by the fire.

It was a beautiful summer's night; our friend's house had a big garden with a fire pit and we had plenty of beer and weed. We sat around and shared tour stories for some time, waxed lyrical about the current music scene and also learned a bit about the wider music industry as our friend had been in some successful acts and toured the world. At some point the atmosphere shifted and the whole situation started to feel really tense, like a bomb was going to go off at any point yet none of us would talk about it. I couldn't quite put my finger on what or why, so in an act of avoidance and sheer exhaustion I decided to call it a night. I presume Rae felt the same shift or was just as exhausted as he called it a night too. Dale, despite being younger than us grew to be streetwise very quickly and hit the hay in the living room. Knowing fine well that by going to bed first he could get the best sleeping spot.

Morning broke, the sun was shining through the loft window and the noise of birds singing woke me up gently. I opened my eyes, fully rested and began to get my shit together. Rae woke up and did the same. We headed downstairs to figure out the plan for the day, figure out how soon we needed to set off and where we could stop for food if we needed to. We entered the living room to see what the guys were up to and Dale was awake but no one else was in the room. This seemed a little strange, but it was nothing out of the ordinary. The dudes could have headed to the shop for cigarettes or breakfast or something. We walked through the kitchen of the house to chill in the garden and wait for the guys to return and we were greeted by our hosts Dad was cheerfully cooking some eggs in a pan. He asked us if we'd like some breakfast making, eggs and avocado on toast perhaps? Obviously we said yes, we were starving artists after all. We were on our way to sit outside and enjoy the view while our breakfast cooked when I noticed that the kitchen walls were covered in awards that our current breakfast chef had earned. Jackpot.

While the three of us were outside basking in the sun musing about what a fantastic morning we were having we thought it only right to let the other guys know about our current breakfast situation. It's not every day you get offered an award-winning breakfast for free while you're on tour is it. The strange thing was that everyone's phones were going straight to voicemail. Not a single one was ringing. We figured they were still out doing whatever they were doing and maybe had no signal, oh well, their loss.

Our eggs arrived with a side of orange juice, hand delivered by the chef what a day! Sat under blue skies we devoured our food, finished our drinks and continued our discussions about the best route to take for the show that day. Dale smoked a cigarette wistfully and once he was finished we decided to begin to get our things together. One of us mentioned it'd be best to check if the van was open so we could begin putting our stuff away.

We walked around the side of the house after taking our plates inside and offering to wash up. The big blue Mercedes was out front where we'd left it. We walked over to the van and opened the side door. We were greeted by Charlton, Metal Dan and the rest of the touring party who were all squinting from the sunlight and they then began to berate us for not coming to find them earlier, asking us who the fuck did we think we were and where had we been etc. We asked everyone to calm down so we could figure out what the fuck was going on. We'd had such a lovely morning up until this point. It turns out that we were right about the tension the night before and our good friend and host had taken a turn for the worse thanks to the influence of alcohol and had gotten really aggressive with the guys out of nowhere. He had apparently began yelling at them and kicked them out of the garden while screaming bloody murder. Not wanting to escalate the situation they all backed off and got into the van.

Everyone's phones were inside the house charging, as were all of their clothes and sleeping equipment. Once it had gone quiet in the house the guys tried to get in to get their stuff but obviously all the doors were locked. So, while we were sound asleep in our nice warm house they were stuck inside a freezing cold van, with no phones, nowhere to piss, no spare clothes, nor did they have anything to sleep on or in.

Upon them recounting the story to us I'd never laughed so hard in my life. I felt bad for them, but I couldn't believe our luck. We all went inside and grabbed our gear. Our hosts explained that our friend was fast asleep, they'd tried to wake him but to no avail. We thanked them, left out the whole van situation, packed up the van and we were on our way. I've not since brought it up with our friend as I imagined he's slightly embarrassed by it. He was going through a bit of a rough spot and has since quit drinking. I wish him well and I am still thankful for his hospitality.

8. The Cockpit - Leeds 26th August 2014

Midway through our career we signed a record deal with Ghost Music. They were an independent record label based in Leeds who had the backing of an American record label named Artery Recordings. Ghost Music used to put on a rather well-known metal festival every summer in Leeds called Ghostfest. It used to attract big metal and hardcore bands from all over the world and had a great reputation. In the lead up to this years festival we were invited to take part in a battle of the bands competition to win the chance to play at the festival. From the outside looking in, with us having just signed to the label it sounded like a fix, but it can't have been, as we didn't win.

To be honest we were happy to be playing at the now defunct Cockpit in Leeds. The Cockpit was a legendary venue that has had some of the biggest acts in the world on the stage, the likes of Queens of The Stoneage, Amy Winehouse, Coldplay and My Chemical Romance to name a few. Like most good venues it had different sized rooms to necessitate different ticket sales and of course we were in the smaller room.

We were hanging out around the back of the venue, drinking beers and smoking weed before doors opened to our show. Frank Turners side project 'Mongol Horde' were playing in the bigger room next to us. Some of his crew and support bands came out to say hello. There was us, the other bands playing our gig and Frank Turners crew all together, talking shit in the way that bands do. Swapping tour stories and discussing which service stations had the better options. At some point Mr Turner himself graced us with his presence. He came outside, introduced himself and hung out with us briefly, then disappeared back in to the venue. Fairly cool of him, we thought. Moments later his tour manager came outside with the venue manager skulking behind him. He mentioned that some members of the bands (who he opted to remain nameless) had been complaining about people smoking weed out the back of the venue. Now, this is England, and at the time of writing, smoking weed is still very much illegal. I understand the venues position and them having to deal with the complaint, even if it did look like they felt fairly uncool making the request. Rules were rules after all.

We soon came to the conclusion that only one person that had gone back inside and therefore would have been able to tell the manager about the weed was Mr Turner. Everyone else was still outside and none of them had even motioned at being bothered by the weed. It's not like any of us were acting particularly crazy, just hanging out, drinking beers and passing some joints around. Plus, the management had come outside to tell us off minutes after Frank had gone back inside. I'm just relaying the facts here, not trying to pin the blame on anyone, but it would definitely seem like Mr anti-establishment himself had told on us. Not very punk rock if you ask me.

9. The Maze – Nottingham 4th December 2014

The date above refers to the time Wraiths had a show at this particular venue, but before we get to that particular story, I'm going to take you way back to being on tour with Hey! Alaska. They had played a show here in 2011, maybe 2012. It was a wonderful summers day in Nottingham, the sun was shining and some of us had made the pilgrimage to this fine city the night before to bask in the madness that was Rock City, the famous alternative nightclub. The venue was situated in Nottingham city centre, so we didn't have far to travel. For some reason today I was acting tour manager, and probably doing a terrible job of it, not that the band needed much except set times and to get paid. After lounging around in the sun discussing the various hangover cures we'd attempted to bring us back to life we loaded the gear in, they sound checked and eventually, played the show. If I remember correctly it wasn't particularly busy, but it wasn't quiet either. We began packing down quickly. The majority of us were lacking sleep and just wanted to head home as quickly as possible. As I was today's tour manager I headed over to the promoter to get the band paid. He saw me coming and disappeared. I hung around asking the venue manager and some other people if they'd seen where he'd gone. Eventually he reappeared and I saw the weight drop from his shoulders when he realised I was still there looking for him and we hadn't simply forgotten about getting paid.

The young man explained to me that he didn't have any money to pay the band. He told me that not enough people came out to the show in order for him to pay us and hinted at the fact that we, the band, had no promoted it well enough. I told him in no uncertain terms that as a band, it was there job to turn up and play, and as his job was a gig promoter, the onus fell on him to actually

PROMOTE the show. I then asked him if he had any other cash in the bank, or in his PayPal account. He told me his PayPal had been blocked, so transfer was out of the question. Mobile banking apps didn't exist at this point in time and so he offered to go to the cash point and withdraw the cash from his account. He explained that it might take him some time, as it's a fair walk from the venue. I told him that I didn't mind, but I'd take the pleasure of walking with him on this lovely summers night to make sure he gets there and back safely, as we were in the gun capital of the UK (at the time) and I'd dread to see something untoward happen to him while he was carrying our cash.

Realising I'd foiled his plan he then mumbled something about his card not working anymore and he'd forgotten. I asked him what he proposed to do and also what he expected us to do in our current situation. We had after all driven halfway across the country, supplied backline to the rest of the bands and played the show. He thought for a moment, then very sheepishly turned around to us and asked if we could we give him a lift somewhere where he knew he'd be able to get the money from, but it's a ten-minute journey in the car.

Instead of piling him in the van, Jamie, one of the guitarists in the band had driven down to Nottingham that day, as he'd had to work in Teesside and drive over as soon as he was finished. So Jamie, our little promoter friend and I jumped in Jamie's Fiesta while he directed us around some very sketchy parts of Nottingham. Jamie and I were fairly certain it was a stitch up and at any point we were prepared for the promoter to simply open the door and run off, but we had to at least try, out of curiosity if anything.

We ended in a rough housing estate on the outskirts of Nottingham. We parked up outside a dilapidated house. It looked like a crack den. He explained to us that he wouldn't be long, but it was best for us to stay in the car. Again, it sounded sketchy but there was no way I was going exploring crack dens with this kid. He walked on up to the house, sulking and knocked the front door.

After a brief moment it opened and he stepped inside, looking back at us in the car as he did.

Jamie and I were in the car for a good ten minutes, discussing the likelihood of whether not we'd see our friend again or if he'd just simply opened the back door and ran straight out of it. We were deciding whether or not to cut our losses when the front door to the house opened. Our friend walked out of the house, visibly flustered and walked over to the car. I opened the car door, step out, he shoves his hands in his pockets and hands me the money. The full fee was in crumpled up five-pound notes, each one was a tiny little ball that looked like they haven't seen daylight for a long, long time. I asked no questions, unfolded them all, checked them under the dim streetlight to make sure they were real while he stood in front of me in silence. I thanked him, got in the car and we got the fuck out of there. To this day I have no idea what he had to do to get that money, but I hoped he'd learned his lesson.

Fast-forward a couple of years later and Wraiths were booked to play another show in Nottingham. By this point we had a booking agent who had organised the tour for us so we hadn't thought getting paid would be an issue, we had contracts and everything. Most of the time I acted as tour manager for Wraiths, mainly because I was the only one who could be bothered and as I mentioned previously the guys liked to take the piss out of me for it. It took me a couple of seconds to realise but as we began loading in to the venue from the van I realised it was the same venue Hey! Alaska had played previously. No biggie, venues often have a multitude of promoters working for them, there was no chance that guy could still be ripping off bands. We unpacked and set up ready for the show. The promoter introduced himself and it dawned on me. Holy fuck, it was our friend, fucked up five-pound note dude.

Obviously I hoped he'd seen the error of his ways and became a slightly better promoter, but I kept an eye on him just in case. The show was quiet, but certainly not dead. There were a few bodies throwing down and we played well.

As the last note rang out I leapt over the drum kit and made a beeline for the promoter before he had chance to worm his way out of paying us. He then proceeded to explain that he'd not made enough money to cover our fee. I couldn't believe the fucking nerve of this guy. All these years later he was still pulling the same shit. Get a new job! You're clearly not meant to be a promoter.

I laughed in his face and he asked me what I thought was so funny. I began to explain that I was the guy that he drove to a crack den all those years ago with Hey! Alaska to get them paid. Upon realising this, he asked me for my PayPal details and transferred us our fee. Moron.

10. The Gryphon - Bristol 3rd May 2015

After signing a record deal we ended up with a Southern booking promoter, which led us to playing at this particular venue in Bristol. I don't know if you've been to Bristol before, but if you're ever near it, then go and check it out. It seemed like the original hipster city, with vegan coffee shops and curly moustached barbers before it was cool.

We pulled up outside the venue and hung out with one of the other bands that'd been on this tour with us. My expectations for the venue weren't high, as from the outside it looked like the only normal pub in an area full of cool venues and coffee shops, but you never know. We headed inside to find we were playing on the second floor of a still functioning pub, which was in the middle of serving food for its guests downstairs while adolescent metal bands were tearing it up upstairs. Bizarre. We bundled through the crowds with our gear, up some stairs until we got to the room we were playing in. It was fucking tiny. Usually we'd love a tiny venue. Fit as many people as you can in and chaos will ensue. The problem was that it was so small that we couldn't get in. We were due on soon and I needed to set my gear up. I couldn't do it outside, it would take forever to get it all up and down the stairs and there was nowhere on the floor beneath us that I could fit in to set up either.

The promoter noticed my angst and pointed at a little red door behind me and told me I could set up my gear in there, perfect. I walked over with some of my drum gear in tow and found a kitchen that was still being used to cook food for the customers downstairs. The chefs waved me and told me to shut the door. I half expected them to stick a tall hat on me and ask me to chop up some onions, but instead they carried on, working around me as I awkwardly set my gear up and tried not to burn myself.

I became increasingly aware of my current personal hygiene, not wanting to contaminate any food with four days' worth of tour grot (we'd been swimming every day, but still). I'd managed to trap myself behind all of my gear, not wanting to get in the way of the chefs while they were hard at work and so I sat on my drum stool, watching them prepare food.

The band currently playing carried on for another twenty minutes while I was having one of those 'what the fuck has my life become?' moments, skint, tired, in a kitchen of a pub waiting to play a gig to fifty kids in the middle of nowhere. Life is strange.

Finally it was our chance to play and the entire time I could just smell the grease on my hair contaminated from the kitchen. It was a wild show though, I remember the guys who worked at the venue having to hold the speakers up because the crowd was smashing into everything.

The next best place I've ever had to set my drums up in was in an awesome little punk rock venue in Sheffield, they had a very cool set up, stage and venue on one side of the bar and a separate side for casual punk rock pub goers to go and enjoy a pint away from the maelstrom. Unfortunately, when designing the bar they forgot one thing, anywhere for anyone to be able to set up their musical equipment. The floor was packed and again, we were about to go on so I had to set up somewhere. I looked around and the only spot available was the disabled toilet. I sighed, dragged my gear over and as I closed the door I looked up to see the faces of my band mates grinning at my choice to be a drummer. The door wouldn't stay shut and it kept hitting people when it swung open, so I had to lock myself in, set up my drum gear and wait for the guys to text me telling me the coast was clear once the previous band had finished.

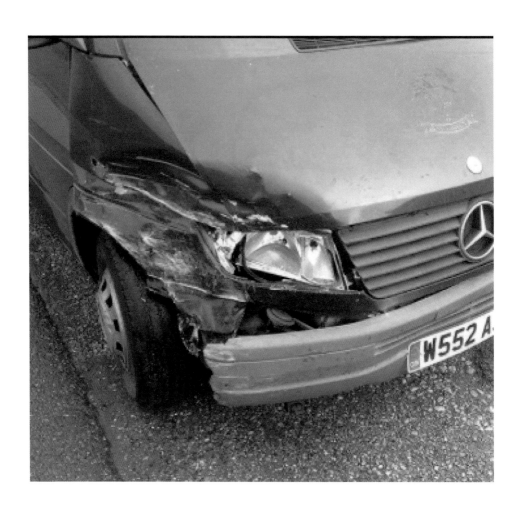

11. Hevy Festival - 15th August 2015

At our peak, Wraiths were asked to play at the rather well respected Hevy festival, which was known for niche and not so niche metal, hard-core and pop punk bands. Some of us had been before as paying customers and we were over the moon to be asked to play. The festival itself took place on the grounds of Port Lympne, which was owned by nearby zoo. By going to the festival, you were given free entry to the zoo, which made it extra cool. We were scheduled to be playing midway through the first day of the festival, which was an ideal slot. You didn't have to get up too early, you were likely to have a crowd of interested people before they got too drunk or tired and you could pack down, get pissed, watch the headliners and enjoy the rest of the weekend, perfect.

Kent (which is where the festival was held) is about as far away from Middlesbrough as you can get and still be in the same country. We were sure it would be worth the long journey and we were very excited to play. It was right in the middle of festival season, which for obvious reasons takes place in the height of summer. We packed the van whilst the sun shone down on us, taking our musical equipment, camping gear, enough booze to sink a battleship and our girlfriends.

After several rest stops and discussions on who we were going to watch at the weekend we almost arrived at the festival site. If you've never been to a festival before, finding the entrances can be quite difficult as they're always held on big patches of rural land to facilitate thousands of drunken morons camping for several days. It's usually even harder for artists because the entrances are hidden to keep super fans from getting up close and personal. We got closer and closer to the festival site entrance, drove past the usual car parking entrance and see the sign for the artist entrance down the road. We pointed it out to our driver who acknowledged it and then flew straight past it. We made him aware of his mistake, but we couldn't turn around as we we're on a tight country road, we carried on hoping to find somewhere we can turn around and head back. It was the day before we were due to play so we weren't exactly in a rush. We came upon a small town and took a tight corner when we heard BAM, felt the van veer off course, skid out and eventually grind to a halt. Shit.

Our driver was sat shouting FUCK over and over again at the top of his voice. We checked over each other in the back, making sure we were all okay and got out of the van to assess the situation. Our view was limited from the back, so we had no idea what had happened. I looked at the wheel on the passenger side, which was slightly buckled but didn't look too bad. I couldn't see any further damage, so it didn't seem too bad at first glance. We all then walked around to the other side of the van to check on Dan when we saw it. A long grey saloon car sat still, it was half off the road, dented heavily by our van and in the drivers seat sat an old lady. The right side of our van had hit the car, our bumper was hanging off and the front drivers side wheel was all bent out of shape.

The poor old dear was visibly shaken. We walked over to her to make sure she was okay and thankfully she assured us she wasn't physically hurt.

We had no idea what to do. Our van was screwed, this poor old lady needed to get her car out of the road and herself home or to a doctors, we were hundreds of miles from home with a busted up van. What was shaping up to be one of the best weekends of our lives was quickly spiralling to become the worst. There was no way we could head home in a tow truck and not play the festival. We'd bigged the show up so much, but we were beginning to think we might not have another option.

A couple of minutes passed as we pondered the potential outcomes and our driver and the sweet old lady swapped insurance details when a car came flying round the corner. Seeing the accident (it was hard not to) they slammed the brakes on and pulled over to one side. Inside were three young men who promptly got out to investigate the situation. On first impressions they looked rough, covered in mud and acted abrasive. I braced for the next part of our disaster story to unfold. As they gallivanted over intrigued in the sight before them, we began to explain what had happened.

They weighed up our current dilemma, took a look at the van and asked if we needed help. Of course we did! They explained to us how the roads became slippery this time of the year due to the heat (which made no sense) and explained how they had just come from helping a friend of theirs out in an accident and fortunately had a car full of tools to help with this sort of situation.

One of them tended to the old lady, making sure she was okay and offered to drive her back to her house in her car. She was happy for the help and told Dan not to worry about the accident, she was just glad everybody was okay. She got in her car with the young man and she was on her way home.

Once the old lady was off the scene, they assessed the van the way mechanics do. They walked round the full perimeter of the van, nudging bits and pulling at parts, kicking tyres and the like. After a full assessment of the damage the two young men walked over to their boot, pulled out a large metal chain with a hook on the end and told us they could try and pull some of the body work out that had been dented in towards the wheel by attaching the hook to the van and the chain to their car while they reversed. We said yes, as we had no other options or ideas on how to fix it. Lo and behold, it worked. The frame of the van grunted and groaned as it stretched out, but it was much better than before. At least for now the sharp corners wouldn't dig into the tyres, effectively bursting them if we made any movement. They took away the chain and with a couple of bangs with their fists they put the bumper back into place. They dusted their hands off and looked back at their work impressed. We all did a once over of the van to make sure nothing else had come apart while we had help, we fired the van up and once everyone was satisfied it was the best it could be we thanked the guys, gave them some of our beers as payment, they jumped in their car and were off.

I was stunned. The chances of these guys going past us just after a crash and having all the tools necessary were improbable to say the least. It was almost too coincidental and I half expected some sort of scam once Dan sorted the insurance out, but nope, nothing out of the ordinary. These guys went completely out of their way to help us out. They could have just kept going, or just helped the old lady out and went about their day but instead like a pair of country folk mechanical guardian angels they fixed up our van and sent us on our way. The alternative would have been to be towed home and cancel our appearance. Yet, here we were, back in the van, ready to play a festival!

Once we finally found the artist entrance we parked up and prayed it wouldn't rain. Our van was running but we weren't sure if it would get us out of any very muddy fields in its current state. We packed up our things, grabbed the beer, tents and picked a spot to pitch our tent. We spent the evening getting to grips with the festival site, drinking cheap lager and laughing about the day's events, so that we didn't cry.

We woke up the next morning bleary eyed but excited. With some food in our bellies and a good nights sleep we were ready to smash it. We got our gear from the van, hauling it halfway across the production area of the campsite because we didn't want to risk getting the van stuck and introduced ourselves to the tour manager. After what felt like an eternity it was finally our turn to get up and play. We began taking our equipment out onto the stage and the tent was full. I couldn't believe it. We were so excited. After we got all of our equipment on stage we bro hugged and downed some beers. Our intro song kicked in and we were off. Everyone was on perfect form, I don't think we missed a note, beat or word for the whole set. The crowd lapped it up and we emerged victorious.

My memories of the evening are hazy at best. We drank, ate, danced, ate some more, drank some more and eventually collapsed in our tents.

We'd had such a good weekend that we'd almost forgotten about the crash a few days prior. As we packed away our tents it slowly dawned on us all that we'd be heading home in a van that may or may not be a death trap, but we had no other choice. As we got to the van and looked it over it was obvious that the sharp part of the wheel arch had bent back in slightly and was facing the tyre. Which meant that if the van went over a speed bump or a large dip in the road it could puncture the tyre, leading to a blow out and potentially a nasty accident. We discussed this and decided that we'd have to take it easy on the way home. We were all exhausted yet completely on edge about the entire situation for the entire journey. Every so often we would hit a bump and there'd be a horrible scraping noise, which was the bodywork digging into the tyre. Our driver would then slow down, but as is natural with driving we would slowly creep up in speed, hit a bump in the road and we'd hear that terrifying noise again. Every time I heard it I couldn't help but think that it was the one that would send us flying.

Eventually, we made it. The best show I've ever played followed by the worst drive home I have ever encountered. Once we eventually got to our own beds I think I slept for 24 hours solid.

Whoever those guys were that helped us out, thank you. Because of them I had one of the best weekends of my entire life.

12. Swansea / Bolton - 10th & 11th September 2015

As I previously mentioned, a great way to kill time and get a wash on tour was by visiting the nearest water park. We used to get some funny looks, tattooed smelly moshers rocking up to wet 'n' wild on a random Tuesday afternoon. Wraiths were coming towards the end of what became their last ever tour. We were on the road with a band called Strains who were from Europe and took gigging very seriously, but they were nice dudes and a great band.

By this point Wraiths had upped their production value and began using a click track with in-ear monitors and an atmospheric backing track that fired through the main speakers. This made our set 30 minutes of pure ferocity. We were tight, loud and demanded attention. We tried to keep the set-up as simple as possible and so I was the only one who could hear the click track. That means that the responsibility was on me to keep everybody in time. If I fucked up and slipped out of time, the whole show went to shit and we'd basically have to start again, not from the beginning of the song, but the beginning of the set.

The day before the aforementioned date in Bolton we wandered into a waterpark to cleanse our bodies and minds. Once we'd fucked around in the wave machine and had our fill of cannonballing into the pool we got out. Upon leaving the pool I realised my left ear was blocked with water and I couldn't hear out of it. This sensation is something that can happen often if you swim regularly and so I didn't think anything of it, I thought that as per usual over time it would clear up. We got in the car and drove to Swansea, our destination for the nights gig.

Once we arrived at the venue, we did the usual. Set up, sound check and chill. With the room being empty and us just needing to test the levels I hadn't discovered the impact that only having one working ear was going to have on the set, for some reason we didn't go through a full song, arrogant confidence probably. When our set time rolled around we set up and kicked off our intro. Immediately I knew something was wrong, I could still only hear out of one ear but I figured the other one would compensate. It wasn't the case. I could barely hear the click track or the main guitar.

These are the two things I relied on most in order to play a tight set. I stumbled my way through the first track and barely made it through the second. I couldn't hear the click kick in to the next track and I missed the count in. All throughout the song we were about 2 beats behind, which meant that bass drops and atmospheric guitar parts were kicking in out of nowhere. This made it sound awful but also threw everybody off their game.

When this had happened in the past we've been able to pull it back by playing an extra-long or extra-short drum fill, or taking less time when there's a gap in the song to rectify where we are in the song, but because I could only hear out of one ear I couldn't figure out whether to come in too quickly or too slowly so we just fumbled through it. By the time the song was over I was gutted, but we brought it back for the fourth song and smashed through it and then proceeded to fuck up the fifth and final tune. I'd given up by this point and around a minute in I just pulled out the cables to the effects pad and we played raw. Which would have been fun but throughout the set I'd began to develop pain in the ear I was deaf in, which became worse and worse as the set went on.

Deflated and defeated I packed down my gear and took some painkillers. That night someone had kindly put us up in Wales. When we arrived, it turned out we were sleeping in what was basically a big shed. It was freezing cold in the middle of Wales, but we had somewhere to lay our heads down. The guy who put us up had also decided to invite all of his friends round to drink and smoke in the shed with us, which was the last thing I wanted but beggars can't be choosers.

We woke up the next day in whatever sleepy Welsh town we were in and wandered around the village in search of breakfast. I remember getting some very funny looks in the local greasy spoon and when I asked the local pharmacy if they had anything that could help out my ear problem they looked at me like I was an alien, so came out with nothing. I spent the whole day complaining about my ear and tipping my head to one side to try and clear the blockage. No such luck.

We cancelled the show in Bolton. We turned up but my hearing was even worse, my head was killing me and we decided that not playing at all was better than playing a show that was just 'okay'. We prided ourselves on our live shows and didn't want to be remembered by a mediocre performance. We explained the situation to Strains who carried on and played the show without us. It was a shame because at the time we figured we'd be back on the road to make up for it at some point, but it was never to be. This ended up being our last ever tour. We played a couple more one-off high profile shows afterwards until we ultimately faded into the ether, never to play a show again.

Wraiths were a huge part of my life and in between all of the aforementioned stories lies some of the most fun I've ever had. There is simply no feeling quite like gearing up for tour, packing up the van with your equipment and your best friends ready to take on the world. We felt invincible and considering what we put our bodies through we must have been.

Honourable Mentions

Before Wraiths existed, I played in a number of bands and became embedded in the local music scene. This led to me having the opportunity to stage manage some high profile shows, tour manage some lesser profile ones and pretend to be a merch guy on some of my friends' bands tours. Some things happened on those tours that can quite simply never be put down on paper for legal reasons, but some of my fondest memories lie below, and in some cases, names have been changed to protect those involved.

13. Hey! Alaska's second biggest show ever - 9th September 2010

My first touring experiences were thanks to local pop punk/screamo outfit Hey! Alaska. This particular show was a multitude of ridiculous experiences. To get this particular show their bassist worked at HMV, who used to run an annual battle of the bands competition for their employees. They'd smashed through the previous rounds and were now in the final, with the chance to win a single produced by Universal Media and play at an industry showcase featuring the likes of Manic Street Preachers and Tinie Tempah. The show also marked the last day of this particular tour and they wanted to go out with a bang. I was leaving the guys in London to head down to Bestival as I'd gotten some work as a cameraman for the weekend and when you're 22 you don't need to sleep.

We were in the van on another sunny day, heading into London when we had a blowout. For those of you that don't know what a blowout is; it's the name for your tyre exploding while you're still driving. It can be pretty scary in a normal car, but when you're in an old van with nine people plus musical equipment it's terrifying. Once our driver regained control of the van we pulled into the hard shoulder and took a look at the damage. The tyre had been completely ripped apart, we shouldn't really have been able to control the van the way that we did but we were safe. After a couple of phone calls we had some breakdown assistance, a new tyre and we were back on the road.

We pulled up out the back of the huge venue and loaded the gear in. I could feel the nervousness in the air. I was along for moral support and to take some video footage of the show. Most of the footage I had of before the show was everybody anxiously warming up without much to say.

The competition was a battle of the bands style performance. There was only a small crowd allowed in and the room was huge, this can be really detrimental to your energy on stage, but it didn't affect the guys one bit. Only because I'd seen them play so many shows could I tell that they were nervous, but to your regular onlooker they were fearless. They smashed through the tracks (they were only allowed to play two) said their thank you's and we waited nervously for the result. After what felt like an eternity the judges were ready to announce first place. They fucking won! They were off to the O2 Apollo to play a show to industry leaders, MC'd by John Bishop, headlined by The Manic Street Preachers and they were getting a single released, promoted and published by the Universal Music Group. It was time to celebrate! We started getting hammered on champagne and anything else we could get our hands on for free or cheaply. We drank a tonne, packed the van up and decided to go out. Some of us stayed at the venue, some others took the gear back to the hotel and some others had already gone to a nearby pub.

I was left in the venue with Hey Alaska's merch guy. He was a good dude, but he had a bit of a weird streak when he drank alcohol, which he did, all the time. I have no idea how I was landed on my own with him, but we realised it was just us two in the venue and decided to try and find the guys in the pub.

I was pretty smashed by this point, but this guy was destroyed. He was struggling to walk and swearing at everyone we see. Exactly what you need in the centre of London. We made our way to the pub to meet everyone and after losing our way more than once we arrived to be greeted by a big fat 'Closed' sign and a locked door. I tried calling everyone and found out that they'd gotten sick of waiting for everyone (us included) and headed back to the hotel.

There was no way I was going out in London with my drunken friend. He was really starting to piss me off, falling over, refusing to cooperate with me and swinging his fists wildly when I disagreed with him, but over the years I've dealt with worse and I couldn't exactly just ditch him in the middle of London. We were about to cross the road to head back in the direction of the hotel when a fully blacked out Mercedes sports car approached us, slowly. I was doing my best to ignore it when my drunken friend looked over at it, slurred 'What the fuck are you looking at' and spat on the windscreen. My heart sank, here we fucking go. They carried on driving towards the green light in front of them while I was dragging my friend across the road, trying to get out of sight as quickly as possible when they do a full U-turn and begin speeding up towards us.

I sped up and dragged my dude across the road, narrowly avoiding being hit by the car. I hurried him around a corner and I could hear the tyres screeching and the car reversing, they were still looking for us. I looked to our left and we were blocked by a wall. To our right was a way out but the car would definitely see us. By this point it was creeping up the road we'd just went down and I could hear the dim purr of the engine getting closer and closer. My hand was over my friend's mouth by this point as he kept trying to shout at the people in the car. I saw a doorway to my left and dragged my friend and I inside it just in time for the car to peep around the corner. I'm sucking my chest in, trying not to breathe whilst holding my friend back with all of strength, preventing him from leaning forward and shouting at the Mercedes owners.

A few seconds went by as the car decided which way it would go. My heart was in my mouth and it felt like an eternity went by when the car decided to go right, thank the lord. If they'd have gone left, there was no doubt they'd have seen us and proceeded to beat the shit out of us for my friend spitting on their lovely drug dealer car. I breathed a heavy sigh of relief, grabbed my friend by the scruff of his neck and we made our way back to the hotel incident free.

By the time we got back everyone had gone to bed and I planned on doing the same. I left my friend in the lobby; as far as I was concerned my job was done and headed up to my room. As there was about four of us sharing single rooms I curled up on the floor and remembered I'd left my sleeping bag in the van. Fuck it; there was no way I was heading back outside again now. I passed out in my jeans and denim jacket ready to say goodbye to the tour and hello to working at a festival on the Isle of Wight for the next three days.

14. Bestival - 10th to 13th September 2010

The following morning we hopped in the van to get the tyre fixed, wolfed down some breakfast and I said my goodbyes. It had been an amazing run for them ending with a victory for them in London.

I had been commissioned by a University to film some performance art at the world renowned Bestival. Bestival used to take place on a huge piece of land on the Isle of Wight. The Isle of Wight is at the very the bottom of the country, you have to get there via ferry and is probably closer to France than it is to the rest of the UK.

Once I'd gathered my things I jumped on the train from London to Southampton. Then got on a ferry from Southampton to the Isle of Wight and I then had to get on a bus to the festival site itself. I finally landed on site just in time to meet the rest of the crew, put my gear down, grab a camera and head out to film some pick up shots.

I won't bore you with the details of the ins and outs of what I got up to at Bestival. In short, we watched some mind-bending acts, drank plenty, worked hard and barely slept. By the time we got to the Monday morning and the end of the festival I was exhausted. Festivals take it out of you at the best of times, throw in a week long tour beforehand and you're done.

Due to me making my own travel arrangements to arrive at the festival, my journey home looked like this: a ferry to Southampton (2hrs) a train from Southampton to London (2hrs) then a train from London to Middlesbrough (4/5hrs if you're lucky) and then home. I was exhausted and I really, really couldn't be bothered.

The crew I'd been working with had (sensibly) made their journey down to the festival in a camper van. It turns out they were going pretty close to my home in one fell swoop, meaning I could skip all of the changeovers and jumping to and from trains if I went with them. The thought of getting my head down for the majority of the journey sounded blissful. They must have seen the idea flash across my face and offered me a ride home. I was elated. There was a catch, however. We had to smuggle me through border control on the ferry. I wasn't on the paperwork and if I got caught then I would be detained. I didn't have my passport on me and I had a killer tan, so it wouldn't look great for me if I got caught. Challenge accepted.

We began our departure from the Isle of Wight and pulled up onto the ferry. The ferry left the port and we could see that inspections had begun. I was told to get onto the very top bunk and hide in all of the blankets. I did as I was told and hopped up into the very back of the top bunk of the camper van. The rest of the crew began to put all of the blankets, sleeping bags and anything else they could find in front of me to block me in. It's not very often that any campers or vans get inspected, but it's always better to be safe than sorry. My co-conspirators assured me that it looked good and totally inconspicuous. I switched my phone to silent and waited.

A couple of minutes passed by and just as I was beginning to drift off to sleep there was a knock on the side of the van. It was inspection time. I heard some muffled conversation between the driver and inspectors, and everyone proceeded to depart the van. I could hear them rummaging around all parts of the van and checking the gear. It was only a matter of time until they came to me in my bundle of blankets. They then began to pat down all of the bedding directly in front of me, I held my breath as I could hear hands patting down all of the bedding in front of me, gradually getting closer and closer to me. I tried to slowly, move backwards away from the hand and tried to make myself as thin as possible to avoid being caught. It got to the point where hands were right in front of my face.

There was a brief pause and I closed my eyes bracing for my imminent arrest, when the hands disappeared from my sight and the inspectors left the van. I waited for what felt like an eternity to get the all clear. Gradually everyone said their goodbyes to the inspectors, climbed back in the van and shut the door over. I let out the biggest sigh of my entire life, patted some of the bedding down so I could see the guys and smiled. I've never felt so relieved. After discussing our tale of terror with the rest of the guys I embraced my new life as a stowaway and slept for the entirety of the rest of the journey. I was free.

I was dropped off at the nearest station and said goodbye to my friends and crew. I was still a couple of hours from home when I realised that I had no money left in my bank and I couldn't use the train tickets I'd ditched as they were pre-paid for specific trains. I was stranded. I was so close, yet so far from home. I called up my good friend Adam and asked to borrow the money for a train ticket home. He sent me it across, and I finally got to my house. I dropped my bags, crawled into bed and slept for what felt like a week.

15. Rock City with Hey! Alaska – Nottingham, 19th January 2011

If you've gotten this far then you've read about some of the previous cursed times I've had in Nottingham, but I've also had some amazing times there too. Most of them are thanks to Rock City, the city's infamous alternative nightclub.

Hey! Alaska had been booked to play one of the smaller rooms in the venue and as per usual I was along for the ride to film the show (or at least attempt to) while getting wasted. The beauty of Hey! Alaska's van was that it had 9 seats installed, so some friends came with us too. Drinking had started the second we got in the van to drive down to Nottingham. Which will have been around 2pm. The journey was a blur, but I remember certain friends didn't even make it to the club because they'd gotten so wasted during the show. Which the band smashed by the way, they always did rise to the occasion. Even if we were plying them with drink while they were on stage, trying to get them as fucked up as possible.

We packed down the gear and threw it into the van as quick as humanly possible so we could get ready for the night ahead. The van was parked out the back of the venue and we left it there, as it was also our bed for the night. You see, the Hey! Alaska guys got pretty inventive with the space in that van. It was like a Tardis, they'd somehow managed to fit nine seats, enough space for a full bands gear including amps and drum shells, plus built in bunk beds that you could squeeze five people into, leaving the rest to pick a spot on the van floor or seats.

We changed out of our sweaty T-shirts, downed some of our own beer (to get as drunk as possible as cheaply as possible) and headed back into the venue. We thought we were big time, and acted like it. Rock City is a fantastic nightclub if you're into rock music. On a busy night it has three separate rooms playing different types of alternative music and is usually packed to the rafters. This night was no different. We got blasted on whatever booze we could get our hands on and threw ourselves around the dance floor until the music stopped.

The club closed around 4am and we stumbled out in the way drunken young wannabe rock stars do. Some went to the pizza shop, some had already hit the hay and taken the best sleeping spots in the van, and others fucked around outside in search of any final drops of booze. When I'd had enough, I went back to the van in search of sleep.

I was relegated to the three front seats. The smarter lads among us had already gotten well tucked up in the best sleeping areas. I put my hoody and joggers on to sleep in and tried to get comfortable. I ended up lying flat on my back like a vampire, which meant I had the handbrake digging in the centre of my back and seatbelt clips digging into everywhere else. It was impossible to sleep. Spinny room had set in and I didn't dare close both of my eyes otherwise I'd definitely be sick everywhere.

It had hit just past 5am by this point and I had forgotten my golden rule. If I stay up past 5am after a night on the booze I throw up everywhere, it still happens to this day. This night was no different, but I'd forgotten the time.

I rolled around in a valiant attempt to get some sleep. I was just curling up into the foetal position, about to let sleep take me when I heard a knock at the window. I opened my eyes and looked up to see guitarist Andy staring down at me smoking a cigarette. I sat up like Dracula rising out of a coffin, maintaining eye contact with him as he blew a plume of smoke directly in my face. The sight and the smell of the smoke turned my stomach and before I could stop it that familiar feeling of bile rose from my stomach and I vomited everywhere. I felt chunks of sick splash back on my face when I realised the window I was certain I'd smelt the smoke through was actually shut. The sick gradually slid down revealing Andy in hysterics at me. I could feel the sick rising again and in my sleepy drunken stupor I couldn't figure out how to unlock the door so I decided to wind down the window. I clambered out of the van window, mopping up most of the sick with my clothing as I did so. I darted to a little spot behind the bins in an attempt to be as inconspicuous as possible, checked the time on my phone, just after 5am.

In between bouts of throwing up I could hear a familiar voice getting closer and looked up to see one of the guys on the phone to his girlfriend. They were known for their constant arguing and tonight was no different. I was chuckling to myself in between bursts of throwing up as I overheard one half of the lovers tiff. It reached its climax when out of frustration he threw his phone across the car park and tried with all of his might to smash a bottle of beer over his head.

A note on the bottles of beer we used to drink; our aim was to get as drunk as possible as cheaply as possible, so we used to buy boxes and boxes of the stuff that comes in small green bottles and is found at the bottom of the shelves in supermarkets. It tasted like sand and because the bottles were so small they were very hard to smash, especially over your own head. Our friend found this out quickly as I heard the clunk of the bottle bouncing off his head unbroken. He dropped to his knees, clutching his head in pain and I laughed harder than I've ever laughed in my life. Suddenly I felt much better. Chuckling to myself at my friend's misfortune I realised I'd gotten out of the van in such a hurry that I was barefoot. I got some instant karma in the way of some glass sticking in the sole of my foot. Yelping, I hopped over to the van, leaving my friend behind me on the floor clutching his head as I opened the door, got back onto my three front seats and passed out with a handbrake digging in my back.

The next morning, I recall seeing the venue staff look over at us in disgust as I brushed my teeth round the side of the van, covered in sick and blood. I gave them a big smile, jumped back in the van and we hit the gas in search of our next adventure.

16. Random Acts #1 - Flight of the Navigator

After serving my time as a stagehand at several venues and festivals around the local area I worked my way up to stage-managing. A stage managers job is to make sure everything runs on time, from the equipment loading in, sound check, doors opening, and to get the bands on stage on time. There's a lot of liaison with the tour manager and you are the go-to guy for whatever the band(s) need. When it goes right, it can be amazing, when it goes wrong you have hundreds of pissed off fans blaming you for whatever has occurred.

A local large venue had asked me to run a show for a very Rock n Roll band. The crew were exactly what you'd imagine a road crew to look like, old dusty guys with beer bellies, beards and T-shirts from Monsters of Rock and other old legendary festivals. Amongst these veterans of the road was a young man with freshly ripped jeans and nice shiny long hair. He didn't say a word or make eye contact with me or anyone else that day. Usually the types of personalities in rock and roll touring are extroverts, so this stood out.

After each band's sound check had finished the road crew headed outside to smoke and kill some time before doors opened. I took this as an opportunity to inquire about our timid young friend.

One of the older guys proceeded explain to me that the timid young man had been a last-minute replacement on the tour as the guy that usually did his job (guitar technician) had a family emergency and so couldn't make the tour. Apparently, our young friend hadn't been so quiet at the start of the tour and spent the majority of their first show telling the rest of the stage crew that they didn't know shit and he was already better than them at their jobs and it was only a matter of time before he left the old guys in the dust.

Needless to say the road dogs didn't take too kindly to the young man's attitude and wanted to teach him a lesson. So, at the end of that night while they were packing the gear away some of them walked up behind him and picked him up, carried him over to an open flight case, dropped him inside it, locked it shut and strapped it into place inside their articulated lorry. They packed up the rest of the gear (being sure to take their time) and drove on to the next show. Approximately four hours drive away!

For the rest of the tour he barely made eye contact with anybody and didn't speak out of turn to anyone.

17. Random Acts #2 - I hope you like Jammin' too

I was once put in charge of looking after a legendary Reggae band at a big, local venue. They have been around for decades and they still put on an amazing show.

The set up and sound check was a rather laid-back affair, something to be expected from a reggae show. Everyone was on time and there was very little drama. The show was sold out which also relieves some pressure; this means that everybody knows where they are at with money and the band are chuffed to be playing to a full venue. The gig started and around halfway through one of the support acts the tour manager for the headline band pulled me to one side. He proceeded to take me out the back of the venue through a side door where we see an ambulance next to the tour bus. He proceeded to inform me that the bassist had collapsed on the bus and may have to be taken to hospital due to a heart condition.

This was probably worst-case scenario but there isn't much you can do here to rectify the situation. A bands health comes first and foremost. There were rumours of one of the guitar techs filling in on bass, but they were soon squashed; all for one and one for all.

The tour manager and I went over potential options and it seemed like the best idea would be to postpone the gig. I'd let the venue management know and when the time was right, he'd announce it to the crowd whilst I briefed security.

The support act finished and the usual hustle and bustle of stagehands taking gear on and off stage paused for a second, which left a vacuum in the air. We decided to set up the stage so that the crowd didn't get a hint of what was going on just yet. We took our time doing so to delay for as long as possible just in case the situation turned around.

The bands stage time came and went, the crowd were becoming more and more restless as time dragged on. We began discussing the ins and outs of what we were going to tell the crowd and the press release when all of a sudden, our 90 year old bassist bursts out the back of the ambulance tearing off a blood pressure monitor spluttering about how if he's going to die he might as well die on stage doing what he loves. He pushed past us all, gets to the side of the stage, put his bass round his neck and turned to us all saying; 'Well, what are you waiting for?'

We all looked at each other, shrugged our shoulders, told the sound guy to get ready and before we knew it, they were on stage. The crowd went wild, all the while none the wiser that moments before the bassist was on death's door.

The stage crew were on tenterhooks for the rest of the show and all eyes were on the bassist. He spent the majority of the set leaning with his back against his amp plucking away at his bass, looking like he could keel over at any minute. Thankfully he made it through the rest of the show and disappeared into the tour bus. Rock n Roll!

Epilogue

More than anything I wanted to get these stories down on paper before I get too old and senile to recall some of the finer details. As I was intoxicated for a considerable amount of it some of the stories even now are hazy at best. The life may not seem attractive to many people, but I genuinely have had some of the best times of my life in a run-down van full of my friends with next to no money in my pocket and the cheapest beer possible in my hand.

It certainly wasn't a regular life while it lasted, nor did I ever hope to live one, at least not while I was young and foolish enough to have the energy to chase such a future. For many people it does work out and the road opened my eyes to that. You can make a living doing the things you love, whether it be playing an instrument, designing merchandise or filming live events (or filming anything for that matter) and you can have fun while doing it. My friends and I are living proof of that. I have more good memories than anyone could possibly hope for, and there's still plenty in the tank to make some more. If you want something, go get it. The road ahead is full of adventure if you just keep your eyes open and look for it.

Thanks

This book and the stories mentioned wouldn't be possible without the aforementioned band members and partners in crime. I'd like to thank Rae, Charlton and Dale from Wraiths, Richy, Andy, Luke, Jamie, Ash, Ritchy, Martin and Tyler from the Hey! Alaska crew, Alex, Adam, Daryl and Ashley (you were basically a member) from Raptors, Razor, Nathan, Dex and the rest of the Demoraliser crew, Gary and the rest of Glass Avalanche, Metal Dan, Phil P, Phil H, Jack and the rest of The Departed, Destroyer BC, Feed The Rhino, Golden Tanks, Mallory Knox, Jonny and Massacre on Broadway, Palm Reader, The Plight, Strains, Ghost Music, Hevy Festival, Alex from Black Tongue, everybody at Tenfeettall, all the staff and crew at The Middlesbrough Empire, Tubby and Knightsie, Eddy Maynard, Mam, Dad, James, Joe and Nat. Lottie for her never ending patience and everybody that ever gave us a floor to sleep on, booked a show for us, paid us for playing, bought merch or generally gave a shit about us.

An extra special thanks goes out to Adam Long and Jonny Grant for proofreading this so meticulously, you guys rule.

Printed in Poland
by Amazon Fulfillment
Poland Sp. z o.o., Wrocław